Table of Contents

Introduction 6
- Part 1: Difficult Speech Patterns 11

Lesson 1: Consonant clusters 12
Lesson 2: Voiced and unvoiced endings for plurals and third person singular 16
Lesson 3: Past tense verbs ending in "ed" 20

Lesson 4: Glottal stops /?/ 24
Lesson 5: Neutral vowel (schwa)/ə/ 26
Lesson 6: Strong and weak forms of words 30
- Part 2: Connected Speech Patterns 35

Lesson 7: Consonant elision 36
Lesson 8: Liaisons – Compound nouns 40
Lesson 9: Liaisons – Phrasal verbs with adverbial particles and prepositions 42
Lesson 10: Liaisons – Continuous verbs with adverbs or nouns 44
Lesson 11: Liaisons – Words with prepositions 46
Lesson 12: Liaison of vowel to vowel 50
Lesson 13: Linking /r/ 54
Lesson 14: Intrusive /r/ 58
- Part 3: Flow of Speech 61

Lesson 15: Natural flow of speech 62
Lesson 16: Sentence stress 64
Lesson 17: Intonation and inflection 66
Lesson 18: Onomatopoeia 70
- Part 4: 4 Ps 73

Lesson 19: 4 Ps (Power, Pause, Pace and Pitch) 74
Lesson 20: Power 76
Lesson 21: Pause 80
Lesson 22: Pace 84
Lesson 23: Pitch 88
Lesson 24: Summary of the 4 Ps 92

- Part 5: Additional Speech Exercises 93
Muscular exercises 94
International Phonetic Alphabet 100
Vowel comparison charts 102
Consonant comparisons 106
Pronunciation of London Underground stations and
place names 109
Pronunciation of British place names 110
Strong and weak forms chart 111
Glossary 112
Bibliography 113
Acknowledgements 114

Introduction

Why we wrote this book

Following the tremendous success of our first book, "Get Rid of your Accent", we launched a series of accent reduction courses for diplomats and professionals. Many of our students had reasonably good pronunciation with a few problem sounds, and just needed to fine-tune some details, such as:

- usage of neutral vowels,
- linkages,
- liaisons, and
- intonation, sentence stress and usage of pauses.

We decided to create a complement to our first book with all the things mentioned above, plus:

- usage of voiced and unvoiced consonants,
- consonant clusters,
- intrusive vowels, and
- glottal stops.

The difficulty with English pronunciation comes from the fact that English inherited many foreign words and names, and kept foreign spelling, but partly or completely anglicised their pronunciation. That's why we also included:

- pronunciation of London Underground stations,
- British geographic names, and
- names of colleges and places of historic interest.

We have also discovered that many non-native English speakers use old-fashioned, outdated expressions that they've taken from various textbooks. Some of them also try to create their own expressions by combining words using correct grammar. That makes them sound very foreign, because English expressions are not based on correct grammar, but just spring up creatively over time and are then copied by others. Native English speakers tend to hear whole phrases, rather than separate words.

All of our students had one goal in common: to blend into an English-speaking society in a most natural way, using good colloquial speech. What we decided to do in this book was to collect expressions that native speakers of English use nowadays. We put them into our sentences, passages and mini dialogues. Our new book will help you to uncover the most current form of this dynamic language.

A short history of English pronunciation

You may notice that the English pronunciation of certain words – especially place names – is not the same as the spelling of the words. Why is this?

Many English words are imported from foreign languages, often when speakers of the language immigrated to or conquered part of England. Germanic peoples, Vikings, and of course the French, who conquered all of England, Wales and Scotland after invading in 1066, are the best-known examples.

When native English people adopted the words, they anglicised them. For many centuries, the people speaking the newly adopted words were illiterate. They never saw, and wouldn't have recognised, the spelling of the words they were saying. So the pronunciation evolved, for hundreds and hundreds of years, completely unconstrained by the way the word was actually spelled.

This is why, just for one example, Worcester is usually pronounced "Wooster", or Leicester is pronounced "Lester". In general, it's often very difficult for a foreign-born person who has seen a place name in print to recognise the same place name when a native English speaker pronounces it.

In the last couple of centuries, as literacy became the norm, some pronunciations have drifted back towards the way a word is spelled. Contact with foreigners causes some English people to try to say words the way they're pronounced in the original language, even though this can sound pretentious. (The French phrase "hors d'œuvres", or appetizers, is pronounced in many different ways for this reason). But place names are deeply embedded in the speech of the indigenous population. So it's unlikely we'll hear English people saying "Warsester" any time soon.

Americans, from a much younger country, were never as illiterate as the medieval English, and were never conquered. So Americans tend to pronounce words in a way much closer to their spelling. But in the UK, American pronunciations, word choices and spellings are somewhat looked down on, and foreign-born speakers who accidentally pick them up often try to get rid of "Americanisms" and return to the original English phrasing, spelling and pronunciation.

Methodology used in this book

We believe that the best way to write a training manual is to base it on practical work, and the best way to learn language skills is by the regular, daily practice of these exercises, so eventually the correct pronunciation becomes second nature to the speaker. We use mini dialogues, short passages, and sentences for you to incorporate the fine points in your speech.

We show how the meaning of a sentence can be changed by placing stress on different words. We use a selection of poetry and prose, where we show how you can use the 4 Ps – power, pitch, pace and pause – to create an impact with your speech.

We support all exercises with recordings on the Audible version and related apps.

Who this book is for

Native English speakers include:
- Pronunciation and speech teachers
- Actors with non-RP accents who wish to widen their range
- Hollywood actors who need to develop a British accent
- Professionals for whom a high standard of English and clarity of speech are important
- Public speakers.

Non-native English speakers include:
- Students
- International businessmen and executives
- Diplomats
- Call centre employees
- Intelligence agents
- Skilled professionals: teachers, professors, doctors, lawyers, journalists, etc, who wish to advance in their profession in Britain, the United States, Canada, Australia and other countries where English is an official or business language (e.g. India)
- People who work in service and hospitality industries and need to communicate with good English
- Public speakers.

Part 1: Difficult Speech Patterns

Lesson 1: Consonant clusters

Consonant clusters can be quite difficult to pronounce for both native and non-native English speakers. The tip of the tongue needs to be tightly controlled in the following clusters.

Do not change /s/ as in "sing" into /ʃ/ as in "shall" in consonant clusters: "str", "spr", "scr", "spl".

A1
🎧 Exercises for consonant cluster "str"

Practise by breaking the word down, as in the examples below, starting the word with the third consonant of the cluster, then adding the second and finally the first.

street	reet	treet	s----treet	street
stress	ress	tress	s----tress	stress
strategy	rategy	trategy	s----trategy	strategy
strange	range	trange	s----trange	strange
strong	rong	trong	s----trong	strong
straight	raight	traight	s----traight	straight

A2
🎧 Sentences for consonant cluster "str"

Listen and repeat. Read each sentence aloud slowly at first, then as if you were telling it to someone in a natural way.

1. Simon reckoned that at a **str**etch, his **str**ategy would put him **str**eets ahead of his rivals.
2. The **str**ong, silent **str**anger stared **str**aight ahead across the room at the **str**ipper.
3. The **str**ength of feeling showed in the **str**ained expressions of the protesters.

A3
🎧 **Exercises for consonant cluster "spr"**

Practise by breaking the word down, as in the examples below, starting the word with the third consonant of the cluster, then adding the second and finally the first.

spring	ring	pring	s----pring	spring
spread	read	pread	s----pread	spread
sprawl	rawl	prawl	s----prawl	sprawl
spray	ray	pray	s----pray	spray
sprain	rain	prain	s----prain	sprain
sprinkle	rinkle	prinkle	s----prinkle	sprinkle

A4
🎧 **Sentences for consonant cluster "spr"**

Listen and repeat. Read each sentence aloud slowly at first, then as if you were telling it to someone in a natural way.

1. With a final **spr**int, the hurdler won the race but **spr**ained his ankle.
2. The hostess served **spr**ing greens and brussels **spr**outs with her roast beef.
3. The lawn was **spr**ayed with water and **spr**inkled with fertiliser.

A5
🎧 **Exercises for consonant cluster "scr"**

Practise by breaking the word down, as in the examples below, starting the word with the third consonant of the cluster, then adding the second and finally the first.

scream	ream	cream	s----cream	scream
screen	reen	creen	s----creen	screen
screech	reech	creetch	s----creech	screech
scrap	rap	crap	s----crap	scrap
scratch	ratch	cratch	s----cratch	scratch
scramble	ramble	cramble	s----cramble	scramble

A6
🎧 Sentences for consonant cluster "scr"

Listen and repeat. Read each sentence aloud slowly at first, then as if you were telling it to someone in a natural way.

1. **Scr**eaming and **scr**eeching in public is not really done.
2. The film director decided to **scr**ap the **scr**eenplay and re-write the **scr**ipt.
3. Simon **scr**atched his legs as he **scr**ambled through the **scr**ubland.

A7
🎧 Exercises for consonant cluster "spl"

Practise by breaking the word down, as in the examples below, starting the word with the third consonant of the cluster, then adding the second and finally the first.

splash	lash	plash	s----plash	splash
split	lit	plit	s----plit	split
splendid	lendid	plendid	s----plendid	splendid
splutter	lutter	plutter	s----plutter	splutter
splinter	linter	plinter	s----plinter	splinter
splurge	lurge	plurge	s----plurge	splurge

A8
🎧 Sentences for consonant cluster "spl"

Listen and repeat. Read each sentence aloud slowly at first, then as if you were telling it to someone in a natural way.

1. On his birthday, Richard **spl**urged on a **spl**endid meal.
2. The news of the couple's **spl**it was **spl**ashed all over the newspapers.
3. The car engine **spl**uttered and then **spl**attered oil across the road.

Task: Read the following idioms and colloquial expressions with examples. Note consonant clusters. Make up your own sentences using the examples.

1. To be **str**eets ahead of somebody.
Meaning: To be superior compared to somebody.
2. To have a **scr**ew loose.
Meaning: To be irrational or mentally unstable.
3. To **scr**imp and save.
Meaning: To economise.
4. **Spl**it second.
Meaning: A very brief period of time.
5. To start something from **scr**atch.
Meaning: To start something from the very beginning.
6. To pull a few **str**ings.
Meaning: To use connections for getting a job, a promotion, etc.

Lesson 2: Voiced and unvoiced endings for plurals and third person singular

A9

Rule: If the sound before the ending is unvoiced, then the ending will be unvoiced too. If the sound before the ending is voiced, then the ending will be voiced.

Unvoiced consonants are made purely with breath, voiced consonants are made with breath and sound.

🎧 Unvoiced Consonants	**A10** 🎧 Voiced Consonants
/p/ – put – /pʊt/	/b/ – but – /bʌt/
/t/ – two – /tuː/	/d/ – do – /duː/
/k/ – cake – /ˈkeɪk/	/g/ – go – /gəʊ/
/f/ – fish – /fɪʃ/	/v/ – very – /veri/
/θ/ – think – /θɪŋk/	/ð/ – that –/ðæt/
/s/ – sip – /sɪp/	/z/ – zoo – /zuː/
/ʃ/ – shall – /ʃæl/	/ʒ/ – measure – /meʒə/
/tʃ/ – church – /tʃɜːtʃ/	/dʒ/ – judge – /dʒʌdʒ/
/h/ – hat – /hæt/	/m/ – money – /ˈmʌni/
	/n/ – no – /nəʊ/
	/ŋ/ – sing – /sɪŋ/
	/l/ – light – /laɪt/
	/r/ – river – /ˈrɪvə/
	/j/ – yes – /jes/
	/w/ – was – /wɒz/

Note: All vowels and diphthongs are voiced.

A11
🎧 Comparison: [s] and [z]

[s]	[z]
Verbs	**Verbs**
breaks	brings
rants	reads
jumps	jives
skips	skids
gallops	gives
Plurals	**Plurals**
bits	beds
cats	kegs
hats	hands
gnats	gnomes
nuts	needs

A12
🎧 Sentences for /s/ and /z/

Listen and repeat the following sentences, noting unvoiced and voiced ending.

1. Sticks(s) and stones(z) may break my bones(z) but names(z) will never hurt me.
2. Sweet words(z) butter no parsnips(s).
3. The most successful performer acts(s), dances(z) and sings(z) to a very high standard.
4. Among his many tasks(s), the busy chef chops(s), whisks(s), sieves(z), roasts(s) and grills(z).
5. It's been raining cats(s) and dogs(z) in London, all my clothes(z) are soaking wet.

Rule: An extra syllable is formed by the short vowel /ɪ/ (as in /pɪt/) in **plurals and words in the third person singular ending in "es"**. The result is that the "es" is pronounced as a voiced /ɪz/.

A13
🎧 **Words**

Listen and repeat the following words, noting the /ɪz/ ending.

Plurals ending in /ɪz/	sex**es**, nois**es**, ros**es**, promis**es**, cours**es**, cas**es**, bas**es**, tortois**es**, sentenc**es**, expens**es**.
3rd person singular ending in /ɪz/	chas**es**, refus**es**, excus**es**, produc**es**, divorc**es**, studi**es**, us**es**.

A14
🎧 **Sentences**

Listen and repeat the following sentences, noting the /ɪz/ ending.

1. Mark refus**es** to buy his wife her favourite pink ros**es**.
2. Under certain circumstanc**es**, the accountant us**es** excus**es** for claiming excessive expens**es**.
3. In certain cas**es**, judg**es** hand down severe sentenc**es** to hardened criminals.
4. In the course of the hunt, hedg**es** and fenc**es** proved too high for the hors**es**.

Colloquial expressions

Task: Read the following idioms and colloquial expressions with examples. Note voiced and unvoiced endings. Make up your own sentences using the examples.

1. **On the horns of a dilemma.**
   Meaning: In a very tricky situation – not knowing which way to turn.
   I am expected to produce the name of our new team leader tomorrow; I just can't choose between Brown or Thomson – I'm on the horns of a dilemma.
2. **Let's run this up the flagpole and see if anyone salutes it.**
   Meaning: I have this idea – will anyone agree with it.
   Miss Jones from the furniture department has come up with this scheme – let's run this up the flagpole and see if anyone salutes it.
3. **To blow hot and cold.**
   Meaning: He constantly keeps changing his mind.
   One day my boss promises me a raise and the next day he changes his mind - he keeps blowing hot and cold.
4. **To be three sheets to the wind.**
   Meaning: To be very drunk.
   Having consumed a whole bottle of wine, by the time he rose to make a speech he was already three sheets to the wind.
5. **Pigs might fly!**
   Meaning: It's highly unlikely!
   When the fortune teller told me that I would definitely win a million pounds on the lottery I thought – oh yes, and pigs might fly!

Lesson 3: Past tense verbs ending in "ed"

"ed" at the end of a word can be pronounced as /t/ or /d/, depending on the sound preceding.

Rule 1: If the sound preceding the "ed" is any voiced sound, with the exception of /d/, the "ed" is pronounced /d/ (voiced).

A15
🎧 **Words for voiced ending /d/**

Listen and repeat the following words, noting the voiced /d/ ending.

humm**ed**, cloth**ed**, muddl**ed**, dragg**ed**, breath**ed**, cradl**ed**, bobb**ed**, us**ed**, surviv**ed**, plann**ed**, listen**ed**, declar**ed**, transferr**ed,** featur**ed.**

A16
🎧 **Sentences for voiced ending /d/**

Listen and repeat. Read each sentence aloud slowly at first, then as if you were telling it to someone in a natural way.

1. The mugger pummel**ed** and punched his victim before he seiz**ed** his wallet.
2. The doctor examin**ed** the patient, listen**ed** to his breathing and declar**ed** him fit for work.
3. The baby chuckl**ed** and gurgl**ed** when he was tickl**ed**.
4. Bruis**ed** and batter**ed**, the boxer lay motionless on the canvas.

Rule 2: If the sound preceding the "ed" is any unvoiced sound, with the exception of /t/, the "ed" is pronounced /t/ (unvoiced).

A17
🎧 **Words for unvoiced ending /t/**

Listen and repeat the following words, noting the unvoiced /t/ ending.

kick**ed**, crash**ed**, press**ed**, pump**ed**, cuff**ed**, fish**ed,** toss**ed**, brush**ed**, splash**ed**, cough**ed**, wash**ed**, pitch**ed**, hopp**ed**, rush**ed**, reach**ed**, kiss**ed**, pack**ed**, laugh**ed.**

A18
🎧 **Sentences for unvoiced ending /t/**

Listen and repeat. Read each sentence aloud slowly at first, then as if you were telling it to someone in a natural way.

1. When press**ed** by the police, the thief confess**ed** everything at once.
2. The stallion kick**ed** out, toss**ed** his mane and gallop**ed** away.
3. At the circus the children laugh**ed** and clapp**ed** at the clowns' routines.
4. The hungry chickens peck**ed** and scratch**ed** the ground for food.

Rule 3: If the "ed" is preceded by /t/ or /d/, an extra syllable is formed by a short vowel /ɪ/ as in /pɪt/. The result is that the "ed" is pronounced as a voiced /ɪd/.

A19
🎧 Words for voiced ending /ɪd/

Listen and repeat the following sentences, noting the voiced /ɪd/ ending.

act**ed**, studi**ed**, hunt**ed**, decid**ed**, paint**ed**, head**ed**, start**ed**, depart**ed**, shout**ed**, point**ed**, desert**ed**, knitt**ed**, chatt**ed**, mend**ed**, land**ed**, applaud**ed**, wad**ed**, hand**ed**, disband**ed**, need**ed**, plead**ed**, divid**ed**, part**ed**, erod**ed**.

A20
🎧 Sentences for voiced ending /ɪd/

Listen and repeat. Read each sentence aloud slowly at first, then as if you were telling it to someone in a natural way.

1. At the cross-roads, the hiker consult**ed** his map, head**ed** towards the hills, then decid**ed** to take the lower road.
2. Having reflect**ed**, the suspect**ed** criminal hand**ed** himself in at the police station because he want**ed** to clear his name.
3. The pilot act**ed** on impulse and crash-land**ed** on a desert**ed** island.
4. The old ladies chatt**ed** and knitt**ed** as they wait**ed** for their tea to arrive.

Task: Read the following idioms and colloquial expressions with examples. Note "ed" endings. Make up your own sentences using the examples.

1. A copper-bottomed case.
Meaning: A rock solid case.
The barrister told the judge that the plaintiff definitely had a copper-bottomed case.

2. A well-heeled couple.
Meaning: A rich couple.

The wealthy shoe shop owner and his wife were known locally as a well-heeled couple.

3. No strings attached.
Meaning: It's free of any complications.

Miss Morris, would you like to come out to dinner tonight – purely platonic – no strings attached.

Lesson 4: Glottal stops /?/

A glottal stop occurs when the vocal chords clamp together for a split second, blocking the passage of breath in the throat. (You can feel this happening if you strain or lift something heavy). It is important to keep the breath flowing freely in a phrase or sentence before words starting with a vowel. The phonetic symbol for the glottal stop is /?/.

In some British regional accents, glottal stops often replace the "t", "p" and "k" consonants. This is to be avoided.

e.g., "What a lot of bottles" becomes: /wɒ? ə lɒ? əv bɒ?lz/.

The glottal stop is often inappropriately used to give extra emphasis to a word which starts with a vowel.

A21
🎧 **Sentences**

Listen and repeat. Read each sentence aloud slowly at first, then as if you were telling it to someone in a natural way, keeping a smooth flow of breath between the words.

1. I ate an egg and an apple after boarding the aeroplane.
2. It's absolutely awful the way some people emphasize the wrong word in a sentence.
3. Oh Adrian, it's unbelievably expensive shopping in Oxford Street.
4. Of all the animals in the London Zoo, the most interesting are the elephants and the antelopes.

Lesson 5: Neutral vowel (schwa) /ə/

The schwa is the most used vowel sound in English. It can be found in many words, always in an unstressed position. Its use makes speech more fluent and natural.

Speech organs position:
Jaw is half open, relaxed tongue and lips. Middle of the tongue is halfway up. Tongue is not going forward. The sound is very short.

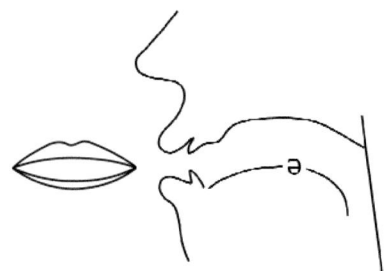

A22
🎧 **Words**

c**o**mmunity, Lond**o**n, eff**o**rt, s**u**ppose, **o**bserve, sev**e**n, wom**a**n, c**o**nstruct**io**n, c**o**nvince, giv**e**n, s**u**pport, doz**e**n, intuit**io**n, driv**e**n, feat**u**red, treas**u**red, wond**e**red, **a**nnouncem**e**nt.

A23
🎧 **Classes of words that have the neutral vowel schwa /ə/:**
1. Endings of names:

Margaret /ˈmɑːgrət/   Barbara /ˈbɑːbrə/
Deborah /ˈdebrə/   Richard /ˈrɪtʃəd/

2. UK Counties ending in "shire" will have [ə] after "sh":

Derbyshire /ˈdɑːbiːʃə/   Hampshire /ˈhæmpʃə/
Lincolnshire /ˈlɪŋkənʃə/ Hertfordshire /ˈhɑːtfədʃə/

3. Names of places ending in "mouth" will usually have [ə] after "m":

Bournemouth /ˈbɔːnməθ/   Dartmouth /ˈdɑːtməθ/
Portsmouth /ˈpɔːtsməθ/   Falmouth /ˈfælməθ/

4. Names of places ending in "ford" will have [ə] after "f":

Guildford /ˈgɪlfəd/   Oxford /ˈɒksfəd/
Stamford /ˈstæmfəd/   Bedford /ˈbedfəd/

5. Names of places ending in "borough" will have [ə] after "r":

Scarborough /ˈskɑːbərə/   Loughborough /ˈlʌf bərə/
Wellingborough /ˈwelɪŋbərə/   Borough /ˈbʌrə/

6. Names of places ending in "ham" will have /əm/ at the end:

Birmingham /ˈbɜːmɪŋəm/   Nottingham /ˈnɒtɪŋəm/
Oldham /ˈəʊldəm/   Clapham /ˈklæpəm/

7. Prefix "St." is pronounced with the schwa:

St. Albans /sənt ˈɔːlbənz/   St. Pauls /sənt ˈpɔːlz/
St. Ives /sənt ˈaɪvz/   St. George /sənt dʒɔːdʒ/

A24
🎧 Sentences

Listen and repeat. Read each sentence aloud slowly at first, then as if you were telling it to someone in a natural way. Schwa is highlighted.

1. Th**e** fast train fr**o**m Clapha**m** Junc**tio**n t**o** Wokingh**a**m is made up **o**f elev**e**n carriages.

2. It w**a**s obvious t**o** th**e** pan**e**l that th**e** sec**o**nd candid**a**te w**a**s streets **a**head **o**f th**e** oth**er**s because **o**f th**e** way he deliv**ere**d his pres**e**nta**tio**n.
3. On their visit t**o** Lond**o**n, th**e** tourists fr**o**m J**a**pan w**ere** very impressed with **St**. Paul's Cathedr**a**l.

A25
🎧 Dialogue: *A tutorial*

Listen and repeat the following dialogues, noting not only the highlighted schwa, but also inflection and intonation.

HE: Miss Mast**er**s, taking all things into c**o**nsidera**tio**n, I don't think you've got **a** leg t**o** stand on with that excuse.

SHE: Sir, I'm not trying t**o** pull th**e** wool ov**er** your eyes – it's more th**a**n my job's worth.

HE: In that case, we must **a**gree t**o** diff**er**.

SHE: Very well, I'll clear my desk straight **a**way.

A26
🎧 **Dialogue:** *Going out*

SHE: Darling, should I wear th**e** red dress or th**e** black one t**o**night?

HE: You look good in both **o**f th**e**m.

SHE: Oh, f**o**r heav**e**n's sake, you must have **a** prefer**e**nce.

HE: I don't really. There's nothing t**o** choose between th**e**m. It's six **o**f one **a**nd half **a** doz**e**n **o**f the oth**er**.

Task: Read the following idioms and colloquial expressions with examples. Note schwa. Make up your own sentences using the examples.

1. Haven't a leg to stand on.
Meaning: There is no basis for your arguments.
2. To pull the wool over somebody's eyes.
Meaning: To deliberately obscure the facts.
3. It's more than my job's worth.
Meaning: It's not worth it.
I'm sorry guv'nor, I cannot let you park in the managing direct**o**r's space – it's more th**a**n my job's worth.
4. It's six of one and half a dozen of the other.
Meaning: It's the same.
(Idiomatic expressions from dialogues)
5. A different kettle of fish.
Meaning: A totally different situation.
You can't c**o**mpare **a**n amateur pr**o**ducti**o**n to **a** pr**o**fessi**o**nal one – it's **a** totally differ**e**nt kettle **o**f fish.

6. To make a mountain out of a mole hill.
Meaning: To make a small incident out to be bigger than it is.
You're making a mountain out of a mole hill. You've only stubbed your toe, you haven't broken your leg.

7. A cock and bull story.
Meaning: A lot of nonsense.
What a ridiculous excuse – I've never heard such a cock and bull story in my life!

8. It's time to grasp the nettle.
Meaning: It's time to tackle a difficult problem.
Now look here, team, this problem has been rumbling on for years. It's time to grasp the nettle and sort it out once and for all.

9. To cost an arm and a leg.
Meaning: To cost a lot of money.
The way things are going, dear, this forthcoming wedding is going to cost me an arm and a leg.

Lesson 6: Strong and weak forms of words

Certain words have two pronunciations. One we call the strong form, which is usually only used when the word is on its own or when it is stressed in a sentence. The other pronunciation, the weak form, is often used in a phrase or sentence if the word is unimportant and thrown away.

There is no consistent rule as to when you would use a strong or weak form. It depends on what message a speaker wishes to convey to his/her listener.

You will see from the sentences below, that we use the strong form when the word is important for the sense of the phrase. We use the weak form, on the other hand, when the word is unimportant and not stressed in a phrase.

A27
🎧 **Sentences**

Listen carefully and repeat the sentences, noting the pronunciation of the strong and weak forms of the word. Colloquial and idiomatic expressions are italic font. Weak forms are underlined.

1. At the end of the day, Linda was right about that.
2. To tell the truth, I'm not very keen to meet him.
3. It's as true as I'm standing here that my ex-husband has a girlfriend who is three years younger than me.
4. It's the height of bad manners to interrupt when someone is speaking.

A28
🎧 Comparisons

Listen carefully and repeat the sentences, noting the pronunciation of the strong and weak forms of the word.

1. Prepositions and pronouns

Stressed position/Strong form, pronounced with a full vowel	Unstressed position/Weak form, pronounced with [ə]
I said I want eggs **a**nd bacon! [æ]	I'll have fish **a**nd chips.
What are you driving **at**? [æ]	I'm not driving **at** anything.
As you already know.... [æ]	it's **as** simple **as** that.
Did you really think th**at**? [æ]	Yes, I thought th**at** it w**as** alright.
What is he thinking **of**? [ɒ]	He is not thinking **of** anything.
Where has she come fr**om**? [ɒ]	She comes fr**om** London.
I would... b**ut** I can't. [ʌ]	We can b**ut** hope.
What are you doing that f**or**? [ɔː]	It's f**or** you.
Have you seen h**er** [ɜː]	I saw h**er** just now.
Is that y**ou**? [uː]	Who do y**ou** think you are?
Where are you going **to**? [uː]	I'm going **to** work.
Is it us or th**em**? [e]	We could always ask th**em**.

A29
🎧 Comparisons: Present tense verbs

Listen carefully and repeat the sentences, noting the pronunciation of the strong and weak forms of the word.

Stressed position/Strong form, pronounced with a full vowel	Unstressed position/Weak form, pronounced with [ə] or not at all
Am I wrong? [æ]	**I'm** not sure.
Can we make this work? [æ]	Well, we c**a**n try.
Sh**all** we catch this bus? [æ]	We sh**a**ll have to.
H**as** he arrived yet? [æ]	He h**as** just come in.
H**a**ve you finished? [æ]	Yes, **I've** just finished.
H**a**d you any idea? [æ]	**We'd** no idea at all.
Are you sure he w**a**s there? [ɒ]	Well, he w**a**s supposed to be.
Are you leaving? [aː]	Yes, we **are** going now.
W**ere** they pleased? [ɜː]	They w**ere** very pleased.
This **is** definitely the solution. [e]	**It's** working well.

A30
🎧 Comparisons: Contractions of the verb "have"

Listen carefully and repeat the sentences, noting the pronunciation of the strong and weak forms of the word.

Stressed position/Strong form, pronounced as /hæv/	Unstressed position/Weak form, pronounced as [əv]
Might you h**a**ve known this?	Well, I might'**ve** done.
Could they h**a**ve lied to you?	They could'**ve** done, I suppose.
Would he h**a**ve done that?	I think he would'**ve**.
Should we h**a**ve left earlier?	Perhaps we should'**ve**.

A31
🎧 Passage

Listen carefully, repeating one section at a time, noting how many times we use the weak form of the word. Read the whole passage without referring to the audio, again, always working towards fluid, connected speech. The weak form of the words is underlined.

"Good morning, ladies <u>and</u> gentlemen,

<u>I've</u> lots of exciting things to tell you about our new product. Because <u>it's</u> so new <u>it'll</u> have <u>to</u> be referred <u>to</u> <u>as</u> "Product X". Can you hear me <u>at</u> the back? I <u>can't</u> speak too loudly in case there<u>'re</u> industrial spies about. I would love to <u>have</u> brought a sample <u>of</u> our new secret product to show you but I couldn<u>'t</u> because the inventor wouldn<u>'t</u> release it, <u>as</u> <u>it's</u> very secret. So you<u>'ll</u> have <u>to</u> take my word <u>for</u> it.

<u>I'll</u> try <u>and</u> describe it <u>to</u> you. It<u>'s</u> quite simply the most dramatic <u>and</u> innovative invention since the electric kettle.

I hope I don'_t_ give too much away if I _was_ to say I'_m_ not sure how we could'_ve_ managed if it hadn'_t_ been invented.

Many of you will _have_ seen similar products on the market. That'_s_ not _to_ say they aren'_t_ quite good but I _can_ state, without fear _of_ contradiction, that "Product X" is streets ahead _of_ our competitors.

Because _of_ the superior quality _of_ "Product X" we _shall_ have _to_ launch a highly sophisticated advertising campaign. _For_ a start, we _shall_ probably need a celebrity, possibly someone _from_ "Big Brother", _to_ front a TV commercial. I _can_ tell you no expense is going _to_ be spared in the world-wide exploitation _of_ our product; and, ladies _and_ gentlemen, when we'_ve_ achieved total market domination, you'_ll_ be able _to_ stand tall _and_ say with pride, I _was_ there when "Product X" _was_ launched!"

Task: Read the following idioms and colloquial expressions with examples. Note strong and weak forms. Make up your own sentences using the examples.

1. **It'_s_ swings and roundabouts.**
Meaning: It could work whichever way you tackled it.
We'_ll_ put both your suggestions to the board: which one will they chose? It'_s_ swing and roundabouts.
2. **It'_s_ in the lap of the gods.**
Meaning: It's out of our control.
Well, I'_ve_ done all I could to win this contract – now it'_s_ in the lap of the gods.
3. **It'_s_ good riddance to bad rubbish.**
Meaning: It's good to get rid of something or someone of no use.
Quite frankly I can'_t_ wait to see the back of him – it'_s_ good riddance to bad rubbish!

Part 2: Connected Speech Patterns

Lesson 7: Consonant elision

In good, natural speech, not every consonant is pronounced. Speech should flow smoothly. When a word finishes with the same consonant the next word starts with, we glide the two sounds into one with a slight pressure hold.

Similarly, if a word finishes with a consonant made with the same speech organs in the same position as the consonant starting the next word, we lose the first consonant. Consonants /t, d, l, n/ are made with the tip of the tongue against the alveolar ridge.

A32
🎧 Word pairs

Listen and repeat the following word pairs, noting that each pair sounds like one word.

hot‿**t**ea, dead‿**d**uck, don't‿**d**are, red‿**l**ion, soap‿**p**owder,

bus‿**s**top, Prime‿**M**inister, real‿**l**oser, with‿**th**em,

look‿**c**losely, stop‿**p**lease!

A33
🎧 Sentences

Listen and repeat. Read each sentence aloud slowly at first, then as if you were telling it to someone in a natural way.

1. Mad‿**d**ogs and Englishmen go out in the midday sun.
2. The horse was too tired just‿**t**o trot‿**t**o Teddington.
3. I need‿**t**o know what‿**t**rain to catch.
4. Big‿**g**oats and black‿**c**ats don't mix.
5. I love thick‿**c**ream with my spotted‿**d**ick pudding.
6. Don't‿**t**ake the second‿**t**urning after the lamp‿**p**ost or you'll get‿**l**ost.

7. Have you had‿**d**inner? If no*t* try some pork‿**c**rackling.

8. Because I don'*t*‿**k**now my pin‿**n**umber I can'*t*‿**d**raw any money out.

A34
🎧 **Dialogue:** *Flat Search*

Listen and repeat the following dialogues, noting not only the consonant elision, but also inflection and intonation.

HE: What sort of property are you looking to rent, Madam?

SHE: Well – in a nutshell, something small and reasonable.

HE: If you said large and expensive perhaps I could possibly accommodate you.

SHE: There must be something you could find for me.

HE: We do have a small studio flat in Surbiton in‿**n**eed of some attention.

SHE: Do you think it would suit me?

HE: It's up to you, Madam. Personally, I wouldn'*t*‿**t**ouch it with a bargepole.

Task: Read the following idioms and colloquial expressions with examples. Note consonant elision. Make up your own sentences using the examples.

1. **The worst case scenario.**
Meaning: All things considered, this would be the worst that could happen.

If we have to cancel this holiday, the worst case scenario is that we would lose our deposit.

2. Not to put too fine a point on it.
Meaning: Without being too precise or pedantic.

Not to put too fine a point on it, in my opinion the man is a complete idiot!

3. I wouldn't touch it with a bargepole.
Meaning: I wouldn't go anywhere near it.

This divorce case has too many complications, I wouldn't touch it with a barge pole.

4. Let's get to grips with this.
Meaning: Let's look at all the facts and try and solve the problem.

We've had so many problems with this project for so long now, it's time we got to grips with it and sorted it out.

Lesson 8: Liaisons – Compound nouns

The English tend to speak in phrases, often linking the words together. To sound fluent in English, liaise words that belong together in a phrase gliding from one word to another, almost pronouncing them as one word. One of the group of words we liaise is **compound nouns**.

A35
🎧 Compound noun word pairs

Listen and repeat, liaise words in a pair, pronounce them as one word.

tennis‿court, football‿pitch, rugby‿match, dish‿washer, management‿accountant, disc‿jockey, sports‿car, golf‿club, tennis‿racket, civil‿servant, travel‿agent, foreign‿exchange, bath‿towel, rowing‿boat, chartered‿accountant, bank‿manager.

A36
🎧 Sentences

Listen and repeat. Read each sentence aloud slowly at first, then as if you were telling it to someone in a natural way.

1. My golf‿coach advises me to take up ballroom‿dancing to help me with my game‿plan.
2. After leaving university, the graduate couldn't decide whether to become a brain‿surgeon or a disc‿jockey.
3. With your breakfast‿cereal you can have skimmed‿milk and stewed‿prunes but not a chocolate‿bar.
4. To book your package‿holiday see your local travel‿agent and order your foreign‿currency.

5. I can't go to the rugby match because I scheduled a meeting with my bank manager.

Task: Read the following idioms and colloquial expressions with examples noting compound nouns. Make up your own sentences using the examples.

1. It's a dog's breakfast.
Meaning: Essentially, it's a mess.
I've looked at the architect's plan for our new conservatory and in my opinion it's a dog's breakfast.

2. To live in a dream world.
Meaning: To be out of touch with reality.
If your brother, with two left feet, thinks he is going to be a ballroom dancing champion, he's living in a dream world!

3. A ball park figure.
Meaning: An approximate figure.
Having studied all the specifications for the new stadium, I estimate the cost, giving you a ball park figure, to be £300 million.

Lesson 9: Liaisons – Phrasal verbs with adverbial particles and prepositions

The second group of words we liaise is **phrasal verbs with their adverbial particles and prepositions**.

A37
🎧 **Phrasal verbs**

Listen and repeat, liaise verbs with adverbial particles and prepositions, pronounce them as one word.

speak‿up, get‿down, settle‿down, cheer‿up, get‿out, back‿off, shut‿up, write‿off, write‿down, save‿up, rub‿off, walk‿away, jump‿off, eat‿up, wash‿up, reach‿out, bend‿down, drive‿away, carry‿on.

A38
🎧 **Sentences with phrasal verbs**

Listen and repeat. Read each sentence aloud slowly at first, then as if you were telling it to someone in a natural way.

1. Don't dive‿off the end of the pier because you might be swept‿away by the tide.
2. The cook decided to heat‿up the casserole before she set‿off for home.

3. You must always look‿out when you step‿down from the kerb.
4. The sergeant major told the soldiers to shut‿up, fall‿out and polish‿up their boots.

Task: Read the following idioms and colloquial expressions with examples. Note the vowel to vowel liaisons. Make up your own sentences using the examples.

1. To go all round the houses.
Meaning: You are going round in circles, not getting to the point.
After listening⌣to your talk on Consonant Elision, I was disappointed because you'd gone⌣all⌣round the houses and hardly mentioned it.

2. Take a leaf out of my book.
Meaning: Do what I would do in this situation.
I know you are crazy about this girl but if you take⌣a⌣leaf⌣out of my book you'll forget⌣all⌣about her and take⌣up golf instead!

3. Wake up and smell the coffee.
Meaning: Be alert to what's happening around you.
This firm is sliding⌣into bankruptcy and you seem to be totally unaware of what's happening – wake⌣up and smell the coffee!

4. To get out of bed on the wrong side.
Meaning: Things are just not going right today.
You're rather grumpy this morning, did you get⌣out⌣of bed on the wrong side?

5. To beat about the bush.
Meaning: To be vague.
Oh, for heaven's sake, darling, don't beat⌣about the bush – just propose and get⌣it⌣over⌣with.

6. To be clutching at straws.
Meaning: You're grasping at the smallest thing to try and save the situation.
If you seriously think that issuing the men with a different colour uniform is going⌣to avert the strike, you're clutching⌣at straws.

Lesson 10: Liaisons – Continuous verbs with adverbs or nouns

The third group of words we liaise is **continuous verbs and adverbs**.

A39
🎧 Continuous verbs with adverbs

Listen and repeat, liaise verbs with adverbs, pronounce them as one word.

Generally‿speaking, fast‿moving, great‿looking, spending‿wisely, thinking‿deeply, wandering‿aimlessly, speaking‿clearly, walking‿briskly, denying‿vehemently, following‿blindly, agreeing‿unanimously.

A40
🎧 Sentences with verbs

Listen and repeat. Read each sentence aloud slowly at first, then as if you were telling it to someone in a natural way.

1. This jacket costs a pretty penny, but because I'm spending‿wisely it'll last me for years.

2. We couldn't make head nor tail of the professor's lecture for the simple reason, that he was gabbling‿inaudibly.

3. Speaking‿frankly, the exorbitant fee you are charging for this work suggests to me that you are pulling‿a‿fast one.

4. Off the top of my head, I would say we're in danger of jumping‿blindly into what seems to be a doubtful enterprise.

A41
🎧 **Continuous verbs with nouns**

Listen and repeat, liaise verbs with adverbs, pronounce them as one word.

Encouraging‿feedback, going‿bankrupt, raising‿objections, swallowing‿food, drinking‿water, cooking‿a‿meal, managing‿a‿company, weighing‿up‿facts.

A42
🎧 **Sentences**

Listen and repeat. Read each sentence aloud slowly at first, then as if you were telling it to someone in a natural way.

1. At the end of the day weighing‿up‿all‿the‿options, we will have to dismiss him.

2. I know sales haven't been great, but in a manner‿of‿speaking, we are making‿money.

3. His first wife was obsessed with aerobics and now he's gone and married a martial arts fanatic – he's gone out‿of‿the‿frying‿pan and into the fire.

4. Gentlemen, this company is going‿bankrupt and there is nothing we can do about it; in‿a word, we are up‿the creek without‿a‿paddle.

Task: Read the following idioms and colloquial expressions with examples. Note the vowel to vowel liaisons. Make up your own sentences using the examples.

1. **Out‿of‿the‿frying pan‿and‿into‿the‿fire.**
Meaning: Going from one bad situation to another.
2. **In‿a‿manner‿of‿speaking.**
Meaning: One way of saying it.
3. **To be‿up‿the creek without‿a‿paddle.**
Meaning: To be in an impossible situation with no escape.

Lesson 11: Liaisons – Words with prepositions

The fourth group of words we liaise is **prepositions and nouns**.

A43
🎧 Words with Prepositions

Listen and repeat, linking prepositions with nouns.

in‿addition, from‿London, in‿town, from‿home, in‿context, in‿a‿way, on‿television, on‿the‿radio, at‿the‿cinema, in‿the‿woods, on‿the‿news, in‿the‿papers, with‿the‿rest, out‿of‿the‿country.

A44
🎧 Sentences: liaise prepositions and articles with nouns

Listen and repeat. Read each sentence aloud slowly at first, then as if you were telling it to someone in a natural way.

1. If you look carefully, from‿a‿distance you can just see the bus stop by‿the‿theatre.
2. Arriving in‿the‿countryside, the final group of‿walkers strode purposefully into‿the‿woods with‿the‿others.
3. Despite being under‿the‿instruction of‿his‿tutor, the student failed to‿hand in‿his essay on‿time.
4. Due‿to‿signal failure, the express train from‿Liverpool was unable to‿stop at‿the‿station‿platform.

A45
🎧 **Dialogue:** *A Matter of Disagreement*

Listen and repeat the following dialogue, noting not only liaisons, but also inflection and intonation.

SHE: From⌣where I'm standing, the situation is quite clear.

HE: Without⌣stating the obvious, I think it needs further discussion.

SHE: It seems⌣to⌣me that we are poles apart on⌣this issue.

HE: In⌣that case, we must agree to⌣differ.

A46
🎧 **Dialogue:** *A Tall Story*

SHE: I can't believe Nigel actually said that.

HE: Are you inferring he was economical with⌣the⌣truth?

SHE: That's putting it mildly.

HE: I agree. He's heading for⌣a fall.

Task: Read the following idioms and colloquial expressions with examples. Note liaison of nouns with prepositions. Make up your own sentences using the examples.

1. Dead in the water.
Meaning: It's ground to a halt.

As⌣far⌣as this company is concerned we're not proceeding with⌣this contract – it's dead in⌣the⌣water.

2. Reading between the lines.
Meaning: Interpreting what hidden meanings may lie between the actual spoken or written words.

Although I received very positive and encouraging feedback after my presentation, reading between the lines, I think they thought it was rubbish!

3. Let's just go with the flow.
Meaning: We'll go along with what everyone else is doing.

I feel this is not the time to raise objections to this motion; I think for now we should just go with the flow.

4. It's all water under the bridge.
Meaning: It's past history, no longer important.

It's no use bringing it up again, it happened a long time ago and it's no longer relevant – it's all water under the bridge.

Lesson 12: Liaison of vowel to vowel

Rule: When a word ends with a vowel, and the following word starts with a vowel, we link them together and pronounce them as one word.

A47
🎧 **Word pairs**

Listen and repeat, linking vowel to vowel.

go‿out, throw‿away, so‿easy, be‿aware, how‿about, stay‿awake, show‿approval, go‿away, go‿abroad, so‿honest, my‿own, by‿and large, by‿all means.

A48
🎧 **Sentences**

Listen and repeat. Read each sentence aloud slowly at first, then as if you were telling it to someone in a natural way.

1. Every Tuesday‿evening we both go‿out to‿our yoga class.
2. Auntie‿Emily and her nephew‿Andrew are rolling in money.
3. He told her to go‿away and stay‿out of trouble.
4. Before you say‿anything you should be‿aware of the effect it may have.
5. Say‿it, don't spray‿it!

A49
🎧 **Dialogue:** *A Dreaded Visit*

Listen to and repeat the following dialogue, noting not only liaison of vowel to vowel, but also inflection and intonation.

SHE: What would you say‿if I told you Mother wants to come and stay for the weekend?

HE: Between you⌣and me⌣and the gatepost, I could think of quite a few things to say.

SHE: Isn't it about time you two buried the hatchet?

HE: The question is – where would I like to bury⌣it?

SHE: Well, tough luck! She's coming!

HE: Over my dead body.

SHE: If necessary.

Task: Read the following idioms and colloquial expressions with examples. Note the vowel to vowel liaisons. Make up your own sentences using the examples.

1. In this day⌣and age.
Meaning: In this particular period in our history.

In this day⌣and age people are far more likely to text or send an e-mail than to write a letter.

2. To be⌣one over the⌣eight
Meaning: To be very drunk.

As the bridegroom weaved his way from side to side down the aisle and then fell flat on his face, it was evident that he was one over the⌣eight!

3. To be worlds apart.
Meaning: We couldn't disagree more; we are diametrically opposed.

I can see no way that management and the trade union can ever be reconciled – they⌣are worlds apart.

4. To hold out the olive branch.
Meaning: Make a conciliatory gesture to make peace.

Our two families haven't spoken to each other for nearly ten years; I believe it's time to hold out the olive branch and put our differences aside.

5. To play it by ear.
Meaning: To act according to the situation.

Since we are not in full possession of all the facts yet, we shall have to play it by ear and see how the situation develops.

Lesson 13: Linking /r/

When the letter "r" ends a word and is followed by a word starting with a vowel, the "r" sound may be pronounced. This helps to make your speech more fluent and connected.

A50
🎧 **Word pairs:**

Link words in a pairs by pronouncing /r/ sound.

        car‿insurance   far‿away
        car‿accident   power‿engine
        under‿arrest   editor‿in charge
        under‿age   fair‿enough

A51
🎧 **Sentences**

Listen and repeat the following sentences, noting that the highlighted linking "r" is pronounced.

1. Where‿are you working today?
2. Her car‿is in the garage all day.
3. I'll love you for ever‿and‿ever‿and ever!
4. We were better‿off last year.
5. My mother‿and father‿and brother‿are coming to stay.
6. I saw Doctor‿Andrews today.
7. I'll have butter‿and jam on my toast.
8. She gave me more‿and more homework.
9. Thank you so much for‿everything.
10. We're‿away in Winchester‿all next week.

A52
🎧 **Dialogue**: *Bolshoi Ballet*

Listen and repeat the following dialogues, noting linking "r".

HE: Once and for⌣all, I do not want to go and see the Bolshoi Ballet! It's just not my cup of tea.

SHE: But they're⌣in a class of their⌣own.

HE: As far⌣as I'm concerned, they can stay on their⌣own.

SHE: Look, I've already booked the tickets. We're going!

HE: Not for⌣all the tea in China.

A53
🎧 **Dialogue**: *University for Sebastian*

SHE: We have to think seriously which university would suit Sebastian best. He's very bright, you know. What about your⌣old college, Caius?

HE: Yes, Cambridge would be marvelous, but is it far⌣enough away?

SHE: Don't be so horrid! Where would you like him to go? Nottingham, Derby, Birmingham, Manchester? Edinburgh even? Is that far⌣enough away?

HE: I was thinking more⌣along the lines of Harvard or Yale.

SHE: You're⌣impossible! Anyway, it's all speculation. After⌣all, he's only 18 months old!

Task: Read the following idioms and colloquial expressions with examples, noting linking /r/. Make up your own sentences using the examples.

1. Without fear of contradiction.
Meaning: This is a rock solid proposition that no one could possibly disagree with.

May I say, without fea**r**‿of contradiction, that no-one else in this company has won more‿orders than I have.

2. For old time's sake.
Meaning: Because of shared experiences.

You and I go back a long way, I know my daughte**r**‿isn't the greatest actress in the world but fo**r**‿old times sake couldn't you give her the part?

3. In a class of his/her/their own.
Meaning: An outstanding performer in art, sport etc.
It's a universally accepted fact that as an artist Coco Chanel was in a class of he**r**‿own.

4. To be up for it.
Meaning: Ready and willing for action.

Right men- we attack at dawn tomorrow! Are you up fo**r**‿it?

5. Not for all the tea in China.
Meaning: However much you offered, I wouldn't do it.
(expression from the dialogue "Bolshoi Ballet")

Lesson 14: Intrusive /r/

Do not put an /r/ sound between words ending in "aw" (long vowel /ɔː/) or the neutral vowel /ə/, spelt "a", and the following word starting with a vowel. It's easier and lazier, but it's not good English.

A54
🎧 Sentences

Listen and repeat the following sentences, noting that a line indicates where you should not put an intrusive "r".

1. Law_ and order.
2. I saw_ a ship at sea.
3. I used raw_ eggs in my cake mixture.
4. Let me draw_ it for you!
5. George Bernard Shaw_ is a well-known playwright.
6. I'll have a soda_ and water, please.
7. She was in awe_ of him.
8. The idea_ of it appalled her.
9. Olga_ and Linda_ are going home.
10. China_ and India_ are on my holiday list.
11. He was given a quota_ of ten tickets.

A55
🎧 Dialogue: *You can't tell a book by its cover.*

Listen and repeat the following dialogue, noting that a line indicates where you should not put an intrusive "r".

SHE: Between you and me and the gate post, I think that Amanda_ is up to something.

HE: What are you driving at?

SHE: I saw_ a man leaving her flat at five o'clock in the morning!

HE: He's probably come to read the gas meter.

SHE: Look, I know what I saw.

HE: Amanda? The very idea_ of it is laughable.

SHE: Well… you can't judge a book by its cover!

Task: Read the following idioms and colloquial expressions from the dialogue, noting the intrusive /r/. Make up your own sentences using the examples.

1. To be up to something.
Meaning: To do something secretly.

2. What are you driving at?
Meaning: What are you hinting at?

3. You can't judge a book by its cover.
Meaning: Appearances can be deceptive.

4. Between you me and the gatepost.
Meaning: Just between the two of us.

Part 3: Flow of Speech

Lesson 15: Natural flow of speech

In natural speech, it's important not to emphasize or stress too many words in a phrase or sentence. As a general rule, we tend to pick out the words which convey the meaning, and lean on them, giving them a little more vocal energy. The rest of the words, we "throw away", an expression used by actors. This often means neutralising vowels, increasing the pace and diminishing the volume.

Task: Read the following sentences and dialogues out loud several times, giving the highlighted important words a little extra length and vocal power. Always make sure the "throw-away" words flow smoothly towards the stressed words. Stressed words are underlined.

A56
🎧 **Sentences**

1. You <u>know</u> because I've already <u>told</u> you that I <u>didn't</u> <u>want</u> to <u>go</u>.
2. The <u>cat</u> who was called "<u>Ginger</u>" was the <u>terror</u> of the <u>neighbourhood</u>.
3. If it hadn't been for the <u>rain</u>, the <u>wedding</u> would've been <u>perfect</u>.
4. From <u>my</u> point of view, the <u>whole</u> <u>affair</u> should've been <u>better</u> <u>managed.</u>
5. The <u>sport</u> was at its <u>height</u>, the <u>sliding</u> was at its <u>quickest,</u> the <u>laughter</u> was at its <u>loudest</u>, when a <u>sharp</u> <u>smart</u> <u>crack</u> was <u>heard</u>. (Pickwick Papers by Charles Dickens).

A57
🎧 **Dialogue**

HE: Good <u>morning</u>, Sarah. Take a <u>seat</u>. Now I've <u>read</u> your <u>essay</u> on *Shakespeare's Comedies.* I found it very <u>amusing.</u>

SHE: Thank you, sir. <u>Actually</u>, it wasn't <u>meant</u> to be <u>funny</u>.

HE: In that case, perhaps, you have an <u>undiscovered</u> <u>gift</u> that you could <u>develop</u>.

SHE: It's very <u>kind</u> of you to <u>say</u> that, sir. So you mean you think I could become a successful <u>TV</u> <u>comedy</u> <u>writer</u>?

HE: Well, I'm thinking more in <u>terms</u> of <u>children's</u> <u>comics</u>.

A58
🎧 **Dialogue:** *Tourist Office*

HE: Good afternoon. I've just got a <u>few</u> hours to spend in <u>London.</u> I wonder if you could <u>tell</u> me what to <u>see</u>!

SHE: Well, it depends what your <u>interests</u> are. We have <u>museums, art galleries, theatres, concert halls</u>.

HE: Well, it's just <u>general sightseeing</u>, really.

SHE: In that case I suggest you <u>take</u> a <u>stroll</u> from here to <u>Piccadilly Circus</u>, and from there to <u>Leicester Square</u>, taking in the <u>National Gallery</u> on your <u>way</u>. There's always <u>Covent Garden,</u> of course, with the <u>marvelous</u> <u>market</u> and <u>restaurants</u>.

HE: I <u>see</u>.

SHE: From there just <u>hop</u> on a <u>bus</u> to <u>Baker Street</u> and <u>call in</u> at <u>Madame Tussaud's</u>, finishing up at <u>Regent's Park</u> for a trip round the <u>London Zoo</u>.

HE: Oh <u>dear</u>, that all sounds <u>so exhausting</u>. I think I'll just go and have a <u>cup</u> of <u>tea</u> instead.

Lesson 16: Sentence stress

To convey the meaning in a sentence, native English speakers usually stress important words and throw away small, unimportant words. "Throwing away" means these unimportant words are not given the same length and vocal energy.

Task: Practice the following exercises, noting how emphasizing a word in a sentence can change the intonation, as well as the meaning.

Sophie might walk to the cinema in Hammersmith.
Sophie **might** walk to the cinema in Hammersmith.
Sophie might **walk** to the cinema in Hammersmith.
Sophie might walk to the **cinema** in Hammersmith.
Sophie might walk to the cinema in **Hammersmith**.

Stress Analysis

By stressing "**Sophie**", we make it clear it was not Helen.
By stressing "**might**", we make it clear it is not definite that she will walk.
By stressing "**walk**", we make it clear she is not driving.
By stressing "**cinema**", we make it clear she is not going to the theatre.
By stressing "**Hammersmith**", we make it clear she is not going to Chiswick.

A59
🎧 **Sentences**

Repeat the sentence, stressing a different word each time.

1. **We** will be driving to Somerset next week.
   We will be **driving** to Somerset next week.
   We will be driving to **Somerset** next week.
   We will be driving to Somerset **next** week.
   We will be driving to Somerset next **week**.

2. **Will** you come and dine with me tomorrow?
   Will you come and **dine** with me tomorrow?
   Will you come and dine with **me** tomorrow?
   Will you come and dine with me **tomorrow**?

Lesson 17: Intonation and inflection

Intonation

Intonation is the rise and fall of pitch **in a phrase or sentence**. Each person will unconsciously copy the speech patterns of his native language or dialect, starting from the time he first begins to talk.

In the British Isles there are many variations of intonation in all areas of regional speech. Compare, for example, someone who comes from Liverpool with someone born in Birmingham. Different languages will have their own patterns of intonation, which in most cases will be very different from Received Pronunciation (RP).

There are books which deal with the complexities of intonation in great depth. We are taking a more practical approach rather than an academic one. In our book, we have sentences, prose passages and poetry recorded in Received Pronunciation by professional English actors. As well as practising the various speech patterns, we recommend that students also pay attention to the intonation and copy it.

The most successful way to achieve RP intonation is to listen to audio books read by English actors, copying and repeating each small section at a time.

Another way of acquiring English intonation is to live in the country and absorb the tunes and rise and fall of the language.

Inflection

Inflection refers to the gentle rise and fall of the voice **in a word or syllable.**

On listening to English speakers it is important to have what we call a "good ear". In other words, to be able to hear the differences in the rise and fall of the voice.

There are six basic inflections, but within these there are many varieties.

A60
🎧 Examples of inflection

Listen carefully and repeat

1. Simple Rising followed by Simple Falling.

HE: Is it lamb or pork?

2. Circumflex Rising followed by Circumflex Falling.

SHE: It's beef.

HE: Beef?

3. Compound Rising followed by Compound Falling.

SHE: I think so.
HE: Oh!

A61
🎧 Dialogue 1

Listen and repeat, taking note of how the six inflections are used in colloquial speech.

SHE: Do you think it will rain today?

HE: It might snow.

SHE: Snow? Oh no! I'm flying to Rome at six.

HE: Keep your fingers crossed.

SHE: OK.

A62
🎧 **Dialogue 2**

SHE: Are you going out then?

HE: I might.

SHE: Where to?

HE: The park.

SHE: The park?

HE: May be.

Task: Taking a section at a time, listen to the following extracts and repeat, taking note of the different inflections.

A63
🎧 **Extract from Shakespeare's play** *As you Like it*

All the world's a stage,
And all the men and women merely players:
They have their exits and their entrances;
And one man in his time plays many parts,
His acts being seven ages. At first the infant,
Mewling and puking in the nurse's arms.
And then the whining school-boy, with his satchel
And shining morning face, creeping like snail
Unwillingly to school. And then the lover,
Sighing like furnace, with a woeful ballad
Made to his mistress' eyebrow. Then a soldier,
Full of strange oaths and bearded like the pard,
Jealous in honour, sudden and quick in quarrel,
Seeking the bubble reputation
Even in the cannon's mouth. And then the justice,
In fair round belly with good capon lined,
With eyes severe and beard of formal cut,

Full of wise saws and modern instances;
And so he plays his part. The sixth age shifts
Into the lean and slipper'd pantaloon,
With spectacles on nose and pouch on side,
His youthful hose, well saved, a world too wide
For his shrunk shank; and his big manly voice,
Turning again toward childish treble, pipes
And whistles in his sound. Last scene of all,
That ends this strange eventful history,
Is second childishness and mere oblivion,
Sans teeth, sans eyes, sans taste, sans everything.

A64
🎧 **A monologue:**

MABEL CHILTERN: Well, Tommy has proposed to me again. Tommy really does nothing but propose to me. He proposed to me last night in the music-room, when I was quite unprotected, as there was an elaborate trio going on. I didn't dare to make the smallest repartee, I need hardly tell you. If I had, it would have stopped the music at once. Musical people are so absurdly unreasonable. They always want one to be perfectly dumb at the very moment when one is longing to be absolutely deaf. Then he proposed to me in broad daylight this morning, in front of that dreadful statue of Achilles. Really, the things that go on in front of that work of art are quite appalling. The police should interfere. At luncheon I saw by the glare in his eye that he was going to propose again, and I just managed to check him in time by assuring him that I was a bimetallist. Fortunately I don't know what bimetallism means. And I don't believe anybody else does either. But the observation crushed Tommy for ten minutes. He looked quite shocked. And then Tommy is so annoying in the way he proposes. If he proposed at the top of his voice, I should not mind so much. That might produce some effect on the public. But he does it in a horrid confidential way. When Tommy wants to be romantic he talks to one just like a doctor. I am very fond of Tommy, but his methods of proposing are quite out of date. I wish, Gertrude, you would speak to him, and tell him that once a week is quite often enough to propose to any one, and that it should always be done in a manner that attracts some attention. (An Ideal Husband, Oscar Wilde)

Lesson 18: Onomatopoeia

The definition of onomatopoeia is quite simple: words which sound like their meaning.

To quote the eminent speech teacher, Wilton Cole, "English is an extraordinarily onomatopoeic language and a good use of this technical means of vocal expression can heighten the value of a word or passage very considerably."

This will particularly apply to any form of public speaking or story telling and make your speech more colourful. Listen carefully to the following words on the audio and then repeat, making sure all the sounds are fully articulated, although some will be more emphasized than others.

Notice the effective use of onomatopoeic words by D.H. Lawrence in his poem, "Humming Bird" (page 82).

A65
🎧 Onomatopoeic words and their definitions

Listen and copy the sounds in the following onomatopoeic words.

ATISHOO – sound of a sneeze
BEEP – sound of a car horn
BUZZ – hum of a bee
BUBBLE – sound made of air in liquid
BASH – a crashing blow
CUCKOO – bird sound
CHEEP – sound of a small chick
CRACKLE – sharp noises, fire or paper crushed
CRUNCH – crushing or crackling sound
CLUNK – resounding metallic noise
DING-A-LING – sound of bells
FIZZ – hissing or bubbling sound
GROWL – hostile, angry sound (of animals)
GURGLE – throaty, bubbling noise
HICCUP – spasm of the diaphragm, resulting in a sharp sound
HISS – sound of a prolonged "s"

JANGLE – discordant, jarring noise
KNOCK-KNOCK – tapping on wood
MEOW – mew of a cat
MOO – noise made by a cow
PLOP – object crashing into water
POP – light, explosive sound
PURR – low, vibrant sound (esp. cats)
PING – short, high-pitched, resonant sound
RATTLE – succession of short, sharp sounds
RUMBLE – deep, resonant sound
RUSTLE – crisp, rubbing sound (e.g. paper)
SNAP – sudden, sharp, crackling sound
SHUSH – sound to silence or calm someone
SPLASH – to scatter liquid
SIZZLE – hissing, frying sound
SQUELCH – sucking noise on wet ground
THUD – dull, heavy sound
TICK-TOCK – ticking of a clock
WHISPER – speak in soft, hushed tone
WHACK – sharp, resounding blow
WHIZZ – a loud buzzing sound
ZIP – short, sharp, whizzing sound
ZING – high-pitched buzzing sound
ZOOM – buzzing or humming sound

A66
🎧 **Passage**

Listen and repeat, noting the sounds in the underlined, onomatopoeic words.

It was breakfast time in the kitchen of Honeycomb Cottage, the home of Professor Stutter (a world authority on the Science of Speech). On the stove in a pan of hot fat the bacon sizzled. Alongside, a pan of boiling water for his breakfast egg bubbled furiously. The Professor splashed a generous portion of semi-skimmed milk on to his Crunchy Puff cereal, which responded with a satisfying snap!, crackle!, pop!

"Ah", said the Professor, as he flung open the window and heard the familiar call of the cuckoo in the distance (Cuckoo! Cuckoo!). "What a perfect day!".

At that precise moment, Cuddles the cat padded in with a plaintive miaow, which swiftly turned into an ear-piercing screech as the Professor inadvertently trod on his tail. Startled, the Professor staggered back, knocking the pan of boiling water into the frying pan, which produced a ferocious fizz as the water plopped onto the hot bacon. Attempting to steady himself, his hand accidentally hit the cereal bowl, sending it whizzing through the air and scattering the contents everywhere. He landed with a squelch on the soggy cereal. "Not such a perfect day after all", he reflected ruefully.

Part 4: 4 Ps

Lesson 19: 4 Ps (Power, Pause, Pace and Pitch)

Introduction

There is nothing attractive about a monotonous voice – a voice which runs along on the same level all the time. This voice is not interesting to others and can never hold their attention for long. The voice drones on without any light or shade, or modulation, as we call it in speech training.

Modulation simply means changing the voice to make it less monotonous to listen to.

We can use what we call the 4 Ps to help make the delivery more energized and dynamic.

The use of 4 Ps is particularly important for prepared speech for more formal settings, where you are addressing an audience. For example: giving a presentation, reading aloud reports and minutes for board meetings, debating, telling a story, broadcasting etc.

Actors will spend a considerable amount of time in their training working on modulation to apply to their performances.

Lesson 20: Power

There will be times when it is necessary to change the amount of volume we use when speaking. In normal conversation, no effort or changes will be required. When communicating with an audience, however, the amount of projection of the voice (or loudness) obviously depends on the situation you are in: how big is the room, how many people are you talking to, how far away are they, are you inside or out in the open?

The basis for all speech is breath. In normal, everyday speech, we use a small volume of breath to pass through the vocal chords to create a sound. When we need to increase the volume and produce louder speech, we need to increase the breath capacity in the lungs, allowing the voice to be projected forward with energy and attack.

Below are a few basic breathing exercises to practise to increase the capacity in the lungs. Before starting them always check your posture.

Posture Preparation

Stand in a good centred position with feet firmly on the floor, slightly apart, relaxing the knees and hips, and keeping the shoulders down, free from any tension. Feel your spine straightening with your head balanced on the neck, as if it was attached to the ceiling by a piece of elastic coming from the top of it.

Breathing exercises:

Exercise 1: Looking in the mirror, take a deep breath, in through the nose, for a count of 3, filling the lungs and feeling the chest expanding sideways and upwards. You should also feel the stomach area move outwards when you breathe in. Then slowly release the breathe through an open mouth for 3 counts on a whispered "AH" sound. As the lungs gradually empty, feel the chest relaxing and the stomach area return to its normal position.

Exercise 2: (to be repeated 5 times): Repeat the above exercise, but this time count out loud 1, 2, 3 as you breathe out, feeling the energy and power of the voice being directed across the room. Each time, always use up all the breath in the lungs. Continue counting out loud as you breathe out, adding 1 count each time, until you reach the count of 10.

Exercise 3: Repeat the exercise but this time instead of counting, vocalise the days of the week in one breath, followed by the months of the year in one breath.

Exercises for Louder Speech

Listen and repeat the following exercises, using the full power of your voice

A67
🎧 Sentence
Suddenly a loud voice shattered the silence. "Halt! Who goes there?" No reply came. "Friend or Foe?" Still no reply. Finally, "Halt! Or I'll shoot!" A shot rang out. Then silence.

A68
🎧 Poem

Cannon to right of them,
Cannon to left of them,
Cannon in front of them
Volley'd & thunder'd;
Storm'd at with shot and shell,
Boldly they rode and well,
Into the jaws of Death,
Into the mouth of Hell
Rode the six hundred.
(*The Charge of the Light Brigade*, by Alfred Lord Tennyson)

A69 Julius Caesar, by William Shakespeare
🎧

"Friends, Romans, countrymen, lend me your ears;
I come to bury Caesar, not to praise him.
The evil that men do lives after them;
The good is oft interred with their bones;
So let it be with Caesar."

Exercises for Quieter Sounds

There are times when speaking quietly can be a very effective means of adding colour to the voice. When using less voice, it is essential to maintain the energy in the consonants so that the speech, though quiet, is always clear and articulated. Listen and repeat the following exercises, noting how effective the use of softer speech can be.

A70
🎧 **Sentence**

Sh! Sh! Don't say a word! Don't make a sound! There's someone coming. Oh no! They mustn't see us! Quick! Hide!

A71
🎧 **Poem**

There's a whisper down the line at 11.39
When the Night Mail's ready to depart,
Saying "Skimble where is Skimble has he gone to hunt the thimble?
We must find him or the train can't start."
(*Old Possum's Book of Practical Cats*, by T.S. Eliot)

A72
🎧 **Poem**

There is a silence where hath been no sound,
There is a silence where no sound may be,
In the cold grave – under the deep deep sea,
Or in wide desert where no life is found,
Which hath been mute, and still must sleep profound.
(Silence, Thomas Hood)

Lesson 21: Pause

The use of pause can be a very effective means of engaging with the audience for the public speaker. For all practical purposes we may classify pauses under three headings: grammatical pause, pause for effect, pause between paragraphs and verses.

1. Grammatical pause

This is indicated by the punctuation. It can also be a useful tool for slowing down a rushed or garbled presentation. If you know you have a tendency to speak too quickly and consequently your audience is confused about what you are trying to say, the following exercise should prove helpful.

Task: Read this passage out loud and when you come to a comma, vocalize "ONE". When you come to a full stop, vocalize "ONE, TWO, THREE". Then repeat the passage, not counting out loud at the punctuation, but leaving suitable pauses there.

A73
🎧 **Passage**

There stood the doll's house,/ a dark spinach green,/ picked out with bright yellow./// Its two solid little chimneys,/ glued on to the roof,/ were painted red and white,/ and the door/, gleaming with yellow varnish,/ was like a little slab of toffee./// Four windows,/ real windows,/ were divided into panes by a broad streak of green.///
There was actually a tiny porch,/ too,/ painted yellow,/ with big lumps of congealed paint hanging along the edge.
(*The Dove's Nest and Other Stories*, Katherine Mansfield?)

2. Pause for effect (or, Dramatic pause)

Pause for effect is used to make a word stand out or to help build up the dramatic tension.

A74
🎧 Sentences

Listen and repeat, noting the length of the pauses you hear in the sentences.

1. "And the winner of the Oscar for best actress is_____ Kate Winslet!"
2. "I don't understand. You mean you_____ love me?
3. "The door slowly opened and there stood _____ Dracula!"
4. "Chairman of the Jury, do you find the prisoner guilty or not guilty?"_____
"Guilty, your honour."

3. Pause between paragraphs in prose or between verses in poetry.

This pause is important to separate different ideas and give your audience time to take in each point before moving onto the next.

A75
🎧 Children's Story

Listen and repeat, noting the pauses between paragraphs.

Once upon a time there was a little girl named Red Riding Hood, who lived with her mother in a cottage by the forest.
////
She was called Red Riding Hood because her proudest possession was a beautiful red cloak with a hood which her mother had made for her.
////
One day she went to visit her grandmother, whose house was in the middle of the forest. She was taking her some freshly baked bread.

////
No sooner had she entered the forest when who should she meet but a seemingly friendly wolf.

A76
🎧 Poem

Listen and repeat, noting the pauses between short verses.

What is this life if, full of care,
We have no time to stand and stare.
////
No time to stand beneath the boughs
And stare as long as sheep or cows.
////
No time to see when woods we pass,
Where squirrels hide their nuts in grass.
////
No time to see in broad daylight,
Streams full of stars, like skies at night.
////
A poor life this if, full of care,
We have no time to stand and stare.
(*Leisure,* William Henry Davis).

Lesson 22: Pace

If you listen carefully to people speaking, you will notice that not everyone is speaking at the same pace. Some speakers' delivery will be faster and others slower.

There are many reasons for this, the main ones being:

1. Temperament/personality/background

Someone who is uptight and tense, and shows signs of being unconfident and anxious will tend to speak rather more quickly than someone who is relaxed and laid-back.

Similarly, a person who is extremely intelligent and bursting with ideas will often tend to gabble as the thoughts come tumbling out.

On the other hand, a person whose thought processes are much slower will have a much more measured delivery.

2. Geographical

Listen to the native speakers from different countries and you will hear that not all languages are spoken at the same pace.

Climate can also affect the amount of energy in the speech organs and therefore the rate of delivery. In hot countries this may result in much slower, relaxed speech.

Compare, for example, a Texan drawl with a pacy, energized New York Bronx accent.

In rural areas of the British Isles, where the tempo of life is much slower than in the inner cities, the resultant pace often reflects this. Compare the slower, more relaxed speech of an older resident of a quiet hamlet in Cornwall with the quick-fire, energized speech of a Cockney market-trader from the East End of London.

3. Expressing emotion.

An effective speaker gets variety of pace by using heightened emotion such as anger, happiness, fear etc. to speak more quickly. When expressing something sorrowful or thoughtful, the pace will be slower.

There is nothing worse, when trying to impart a great deal of information to your audience (whether in a business meeting, a lecture room, a court of law or in a recording studio), than discovering that because you are speaking so quickly, very little of this information is being understood. Often the first thing that happens when a speaker is nervous and not at ease, is that he tends to gabble.

It is always better to concentrate on speaking more slowly when addressing an audience, particularly if you are not speaking in your native tongue.

Fast pace exercise: Listen and repeat the following examples, a small section at a time. Take care with your articulation when using the fast pace, to make your speech clear and crisp.

A77
🎧 **Sentence**

1."How dare you talk to me like this - I've told you before I'll not stand for this sort of behaviour from you or from anyone - get out of my sight immediately."

A78
🎧 **Poem**

And ere three shrill notes the pipe uttered,
You heard as if an army muttered;
And the muttering grew to a grumbling;
And the grumbling grew to a mighty rumbling;
And out of the houses the rats came tumbling.
Great rats, small rats, lean rats, brawny rats,
Brown rats, black rats, gray rats, tawny rats,
Grave old plodders, gay young friskers,
Fathers, mothers, uncles, cousins,

Cocking tails and pricking whiskers,
Families by tens and dozens,
Brothers, sisters, husbands, wives-
Followed the piper for their lives.
(*The Pied Piper of Hamlyn*, Robert Browning)

Slow pace exercise: Listen and repeat the following examples, a small section at a time. Use the punctuation to slow yourself down.

A79
🎧 Sentences

"As I gaze now across the still, silent waters of the lake, my mind drifts back to happier times, when he and I were young. Now it's no longer us - it's only me and instead of happiness, an almost overwhelming sense of loss envelops me. I cannot bear to stay here a moment longer."

A80
🎧 Poem

REMEMBER me when I am gone away,
Gone far away into the silent land;
When you can no more hold me by the hand,
Nor I half turn to go, yet turning stay.
Remember me when no more day by day
You tell me of our future that you plann'd:
Only remember me; you understand
It will be late to counsel then or pray.
Yet if you should forget me for a while
And afterwards remember, do not grieve:
For if the darkness and corruption leave
A vestige of the thoughts that once I had,
Better by far you should forget and smile
Than that you should remember and be sad.

(Christina Georgina Rossetti)

Lesson 23: Pitch

No two speakers will have the same pitch level. By that, we mean speaking with a higher or lower voice.

A child's voice is naturally much higher than an adult's, and when he or she reaches puberty, the pitch will start to drop. In the case of a boy, this can be very sudden, when his voice breaks. With girls it will be a gradual change. With the approach to old age often the pitch will start to rise again as the lung power decreases.

The pitch of the voice changes with different emotions. For example, when a speaker is expressing anger, excitement or surprise the pitch will rise, but when expressing deep, sensitive, sorrowful feelings the pitch will fall.

For the public speaker, it's important to use pitch changes to hold the attention of your audience. There is nothing more boring than listening to someone droning in a monotone.

Below are some technical reasons for changing the pitch:

1. **When starting a new paragraph or a new thought, lift the pitch slightly.**
2. **When reading poetry aloud, lift the pitch slightly when starting a new verse.**
3. **Slightly lower the pitch when using parentheses.**

The human voice has a possible pitch range of over two octaves. That is between sixteen and twenty white consecutive notes on a keyboard. Of course, we very rarely use all these notes but it's possible for a speaker to increase his pitch range with exercises.

Extending pitch range exercises

Exercise 1: Starting on your highest possible note, repeat the word "kitty" as you gradually come down in pitch passing your comfortable natural level and continuing down until you can go no further. Repeat, starting at your lowest note and using the word "giddy" gradually working your way up until you can go no higher. Aim for approximately 16 words each way.

Exercise 2: Work with the phrase: "I'm so excited!". Gradually getting faster, start at your normal pitch level and repeat this sentence five times as you extend the pitch upwards, as far as you can comfortably go.

Exercise 3: Work with the phrase: "I'm really upset". Gradually getting slower, start on your normal pitch level and repeat this sentence five times as you extend the pitch downwards, as far as you can comfortably go.

A81
🎧 **Sentences**

Listen and repeat, noting how pitch can vary to create mood and atmosphere variety.

You've been to see Ben, haven't you? What did he tell you? It's something wonderful, I know it is. He is coming to see me, isn't he? Isn't he? What? Oh, no, that's terrible. I can't believe it. It just doesn't make sense. He was so full of life.

A82
🎧 **Poem**

Listen and repeat, noting how pitch can vary to create mood and atmosphere.

The land's sharp features seemed to be
The Century's corpse outleant,
His crypt the cloudy canopy,
The wind his death-lament.

The ancient pulse of germ and birth
Was shrunken hard and dry,
And every spirit upon earth
Seemed fervourless as I.

At once a voice arose among
The bleak twigs overhead
In a full-hearted evensong
Of joy illimited;
An aged thrush, frail, gaunt, and small,
In blast-beruffled plume,
Had chosen thus to fling his soul
Upon the growing gloom.
(*The Darkling Thrush*, by Thomas Hardy)

A83
🎧 Poem

Listen and repeat, noting how pitch can vary to create mood and atmosphere.

Everyone suddenly burst out singing;
And I was filled with such delight
As prisoned birds must find in freedom
Winging wildly across the white
Orchards and dark green fields, on, on,
And out of sight.
(*Everyone Sang,* Siegfried Sassoon)

Lesson 24: Summary of the 4 Ps

We have dealt with each of the 4 Ps separately and given you examples to practise.

In the following poem, "Humming Bird", the speaker uses all the 4 Ps to create mood and atmosphere , thus making it more interesting for the listener.

A84
 Poem

Listen and repeat, using changes of pitch, pace, power and pause.

I can imagine, in some other world,
Primeval-dumb, far back
In that most awful stillness, that only gasped and hummed,
Humming-birds raced down the avenues.

Before anything had a soul,
While life was a heave of matter, half inanimate,
This little bit chipped off in brilliance
And went whizzing through the slow, vast, succulent stems.

I believe there were no flowers then,
In the world where the humming-bird flashed ahead of creation.
I believe he pierced the slow vegetable veins with his long beak.

Probably he was big
As mosses, and little lizards, they say, were once big.
Probably he was a jabbing, terrifying monster.

We look at him through the wrong end of the long telescope of Time,
Luckily for us.
(*Humming Bird*, by D.H. Lawrence)

Part 5: Additional Speech Exercises

Muscular exercises

The following exercises should be practised on a regular daily basis. This will help to strengthen and give flexibility to the speech organs and ultimately to ensure better articulation and clearer speech.

Tongue exercises

All exercises to be repeated 4 times.

1. Point the tongue, holding it still. Then relax the tongue back in the mouth.

2. Point the tongue. Circle very slowly once to right. Repeat to left.

3. Point the tongue. Circle 3 times quickly to right. Then left.

4. Stretch the tongue towards the nose, then the chin.

5. With tip of tongue behind bottom teeth, push back of tongue forwards and backwards.

6. Flick pointed tongue sideways, touching corners of lips. Gradually quicken.

7. Tap tip of the tongue against alveolar (teeth) ridge. Repeat and quicken.

8. Finish off with rhythm exercises for /t/, /d/, /l/, /k/, /g/.

Tap tongue tip against alveolar ridge.

B1

🎧 *Repeat once from left to right. Do the same for /d/ and /l/ sounds.*

t	t	t	t
tt	tt	tt	t
ttt	ttt	ttt	t
tttt	tttt	tttt	t

Tap the back of the tongue on soft palate
(keeping tongue tip behind bottom teeth)

B2

🎧 *Repeat once from left to right. Do the same for /g/ sound.*

k	k	k	k
kk	kk	kk	k
kkk	kkk	kkk	k
kkkk	kkkk	kkkk	k

Lip exercises

All exercises to be repeated 4 times.

1. With jaw closed, spread lips back to a broad smile, and then bring forward to a tight [uː] position as in "June".

2. Repeat exercise 1, but with jaw open about 1" (2.5 cm).

3. Make a chewing motion in all directions.

4. Keeping the bottom lip still, raise top lip towards nostrils. Bring lips together again. Quicken.

5. Keeping top lip still, move bottom lip down. Bring lips together again. Quicken.

6. Move top and bottom lips alternately. Quicken.

7. To relax the lips, blow through them very gently.

8. Finish off with rhythm exercises for [p], [b], [m] and [w] sounds.

B3

🎧 *Repeat once from left to right. Do the same for /b, m, w/ sound.*

p	p	p	p
pp	pp	pp	p
ppp	ppp	ppp	p
pppp	pppp	pppp	p

RP Exercises

B4

🎧 *Put consonants /p, b, t, d, k, g/ in front of the following six vowel sounds. Repeat once from left to right.*

/uː/ /əʊ/ /ɔː/ /ɑː/ /eɪ/ /iː/

/puː/ /pəʊ/ /pɔː/ /pɑː/ /peɪ/ /piː/
/buː/ /bəʊ/ /bɔː/ /bɑː/ /beɪ/ /biː/
/tuː/ /təʊ/ /tɔː/ /tɑː/ /teɪ/ /tiː/
/duː/ /dəʊ/ /dɔː/ /dɑː/ /deɪ/ /diː/
/kuː/ /kəʊ/ /kɔː/ /kɑː/ /keɪ/ /kiː/
/guː/ /gəʊ/ /gɔː/ /gɑː/ /geɪ/ /giː/

B5

🎧 *Put consonants /p, b, t, d, k, g/ after six vowel sounds. Repeat once from left to right.*

/uːp/ /əʊp/ /ɔːp/ /ɑːp/ /eɪp/ /iːp/
/uːb/ /əʊb/ /ɔːb/ /ɑːb/ /eɪb/ /iːb/
/uːt/ /əʊt/ /ɔːt/ /ɑːt/ /eɪt/ /iːt/
/uːd/ /əʊd/ /ɔːd/ /ɑːd/ /eɪd/ /iːd/
/uːk/ /əʊk/ /ɔːk/ /ɑːk/ /eɪk/ /iːk/
/uːg/ /əʊg/ /ɔːg/ /ɑːg/ /eɪg/ /iːg/

B6

🎧 *Put consonants /p, b, t, d, k, g/ in front of, and after six vowel sounds. Repeat once from left to right.*

/puːp/ /pəʊp/ /pɔːp/ /paːp/ /peɪp/ /piːp/
/buːb/ /bəʊb/ /bɔːb/ /baːb/ /beɪb/ /biːb/
/tuːt/ /təʊt/ /tɔːt/ /taːt/ /teɪt/ /tiːt/
/duːd/ /dəʊd/ /dɔːd/ /daːd/ /deɪd/ /diːd/
/kuːk/ /kəʊk/ /kɔːk/ /kaːk/ /keɪk/ /kiːk/
/guːg/ /gəʊg/ /gɔːg/ /gaːg/ /geɪg/ /giːg/

B7

🎧 *Repeat the following combination of consonants and vowels three times.*

uːst– stuː   əʊst– stəʊ   ɔːst– stɔː   aːst–staː   eɪst– steɪ   iːst– stiː
uːkt– tuː   əʊkt– təʊ   ɔːkt– tɔː   aːkt – taː   eɪkt– teɪ   iːkt– tiː

Articulation Exercises

B8 Poem
🎧

Whisper the following poems once, then repeat slowly with vocalized energy.

To sit in solemn silence in a dull, dark dock,
In a pestilential prison with a life long lock,
Awaiting the sensation of a short, sharp shock,
From a cheap and chippy chopper on a big, black block.
(W.S Gilbert)

B9
🎧 **Poem: The nightmare song**

Whisper the following passages once. Then repeat slowly with vocalized energy.

You're a regular wreck with a crick in your neck,

And no wonder you snore, for your head's on the floor,
And you've needles and pins from your soles to your shins,
And your flesh is a creep, for your left leg's asleep,
And you've cramp in your toes, and a fly on your nose,
And some fluff in your lung, and a feverish tongue,
And a thirst that's intense, and a general sense
That you haven't been sleeping in clover;
But the darkness has passed, and it's daylight at last,
And the night has been long – ditto ditto my song –
And thank goodness they're both over!
(W.S. Gilbert)

International Phonetic Alphabet

B10
🎧 Long Pure Vowels
/iː/ - feet - /fiːt/
/ɜː/ – third – /θɜːd/
/uː/ – boot – /buːt/
/ɑː/ - bark – /bɑːk/
/ɔː/ – fort – /fɔːt/

B11
🎧 Short Pure Vowels
/ɪ/ – pit – /pɪt/
/e/ – pet – /pet/
/æ/ – mad – /mæd/
/ʌ/ – hut – /hʌt/
/ɒ/ – box – /bɒks/
/ʊ/ – book – /bʊk/

Neutral Vowel (schwa)
/ə/ – the – /ðə/

B12
🎧 Diphthongs
/ɪə/ – hear – /hɪə/
/eɪ/ – pay – /peɪ/
/eə/ – pair – /peə/
/aɪ/ – pie – /paɪ/
/aʊ/ – how – /haʊ/
/əʊ/ – boat – /bəʊt/
/ɔɪ/ – boy – /bɔɪ/
/ʊə/ – sewer – /sʊə/

B13/A9
🎧 **Unvoiced Consonants**

/p/ – put – /pʊt/
/t/ – two – /tuː/
/k/ – cake – /keɪk/
/f/ – fish – /fɪʃ/
/θ/ – think – /θɪŋk/
/s/ – sip – /sɪp/
/ʃ/ – shall – /ʃæl/
/tʃ/ – church – /tʃɜːtʃ/
/h/ – hat – /hæt/

B14/A10
🎧 **Voiced Consonants**

/b/ – but – /bʌt/
/d/ – do – /duː/
/g/ – go – /gəʊ/
/v/ – very – /veri/
/ð/ – that – /ðæt/
/z/ – zoo – /zuː/
/ʒ/ – measure – /meʒə/
/dʒ/ – judge – /dʒʌdʒ/

/m/ – money – /ˈmʌni/
/n/ – no – /nəʊ/
/ŋ/ – sing – /sɪŋ/
/l/ – light – /laɪt/
/r/ – river – /ˈrɪvə/
/j/ – yes – /jes/
/w/ – was – /wɒz/

Vowel comparison charts

B15

Listen and repeat word pairs, noting the contrast between the two sounds.

uː	ʊ
c**oo**l	b**oo**k
t**wo**	w**ou**ld
ch**ew**	p**u**ll
r**u**de	s**u**gar
sh**oe**	p**u**t
l**o**se	c**ou**ld
m**o**ve	b**u**tcher
b**eau**tiful	p**u**dding
st**u**pid	c**oo**king
t**o**mb	g**oo**d
t**u**ne	W**orce**ster
m**u**sic	sh**ou**ld

B16

Listen and repeat word pairs, noting the contrast between the two sounds.

ɔː	ɒ
f**our**	**o**ffice
awful	wh**a**t
order	**o**live
bef**ore**	**o**ff
l**aw**	w**a**nder
w**all**	h**o**nest
s**aw**	kn**ow**ledge
ch**or**d	**o**ften
b**ough**t	**o**bstacle
ch**al**k	b**o**mb
th**ough**t	d**o**ctor
ought	c**o**mic

B17
🎧

Listen and repeat word pairs, noting the contrast between the two sounds.

ɑː	ʌ
gr**a**ss	b**u**s
ex**a**mple	b**u**t
s**er**geant	c**ou**ntry
after	d**o**ne
ch**a**ncellor	d**ou**ble
l**au**gh	**o**nion
f**a**st	st**o**mach
d**a**nce	**o**ven
dem**a**nd	L**o**ndon
pl**a**ster	m**o**ney
c**a**n't	w**o**rry
tom**a**to	fr**o**nt

B18
🎧

Listen and repeat word pairs, noting the contrast between the two sounds.

æ	e
b**a**nd	n**e**ck
pl**a**stic	**e**cho
ch**a**racter	**e**mpty
m**a**rry	**a**nyone
actual	m**a**ny
anxiety	s**a**ys
active	d**ea**th
m**a**d	ch**e**que
n**a**p	k**e**ttle
h**a**mmer	n**e**ver
g**a**ther	d**ea**d
b**a**g	Ch**e**lsea

B19

Listen and repeat word pairs, noting the contrast between the two sounds.

ɜː	ə
p**ur**pose	p**u**rsue
c**ur**l	**a**bout
s**ur**geon	sist**er**
sk**ir**t	p**o**tato
S**ir**	b**a**lloon
dist**ur**b	b**a**nan**a**
w**or**ld	c**o**nceive
w**or**d	c**o**nvey
w**or**se	dipl**o**mat
w**or**k	fig**ure**
n**ur**se	p**o**lice
early	eff**or**t

B20

Listen and repeat word pairs, noting the contrast between the two sounds.

iː	ɪ
f**ee**t	p**i**t
th**e**se	l**i**ttle
pl**ea**se	g**i**ve
thr**ee**	Ch**i**sw**i**ck
ch**ea**t	b**i**sc**ui**t
gr**ee**n	g**i**n
sc**e**ne	**I**ndian
p**eo**ple	cabb**a**ge
r**ea**ch	k**i**n
q**uay**	h**y**mn
evening	r**e**ceive
n**ee**d	s**y**ndrome

Consonant comparisons

In our experience we have found that many students have difficulty with certain English consonants. Very often they replace them with consonants which are easier to pronounce. The following comparison charts cover the main problems that foreign speakers have experienced.

B21

Listen and repeat from left to right, noting the different lip and tongue positions.

/b/ but	/v/ very	/w/ was
Lips come together, voiced	Top teeth on bottom lip, voiced	Forward lips pulled back quickly, voiced
bet	**v**et	**w**et
best	**v**est	**w**est
bale	**v**eil	**w**hale
bile	**v**ile	**w**hile
bent	**v**ent	**w**ent
bin	**v**eal	**w**in
mar**b**le	mar**v**el	mar**qu**is

B22

Listen and repeat from left to right, noting the different tongue positions.

/l/ light	/r/ river
Tip of tongue on alveolar ridge, voiced	Tip of tongue curling back behind alveolar ridge, voiced
lot	**r**ot
lo**ll**y	**l**o**rr**y
load	**r**oad
leader	**r**eader
lace	**r**ace
eventua**ll**y	commenta**r**y
actua**ll**y	g**r**oce**r**y
woo**l**y	wo**rr**y
so**l**id	so**rr**y

B23

Listen and repeat from left to right, noting the different lip and tongue positions.

/θ/ **think**	/t/ **two**	/f/ **friend**
Tip of tongue between top and bottom teeth, unvoiced	Tip of tongue on alveolar ridge, unvoiced	Top teeth on bottom lip, unvoiced
thick	**t**ick	**f**reak
thank	**t**ank	**f**rank
three	**t**ree	**f**ree
thatcher	**t**rash	**f**resh
thin	**t**in	**f**in
thread	**t**read	**f**riend
mou**th**	scou**t**	loa**f**
thinker	**t**imber	**f**inger

B24

Listen and repeat from left to right, noting the different lip and tongue positions.

/ð/ **that**	/d/ **do**	/v/ **vend**
Tip of tongue between top and bottom teeth, voiced	Tip of tongue on alveolar ridge, voiced	Top teeth on bottom lip, voiced
there	**d**are	**V**era
they	**d**ay	**v**ain
though	**d**ough	**v**olume
wi**th**	wa**d**	**V**i**v**ien
brea**th**e	brea**d**	bra**v**e
ei**th**er	I**d**a	I**v**y
lea**th**er	la**dd**er	la**v**ish
fea**th**er	fee**d**er	fe**v**er

B25

Listen and repeat from left to right, noting the different tongue positions.

/θ/ think	/s/ sip
Tip of tongue between top and bottom teach, unvoiced	Tip of tongue nearly touching alveolar ridge, unvoiced
think	sink
thought	sort
thing	sing
thin	sin
thumb	sum
thorough	sorrow
truth	truce
cloth	gloss

B26

Listen and repeat from left to right, noting the different tongue positions.

/ð/ that	/z/ oo
Tip of tongue between top and bottom teach, voiced	Tip of tongue nearly touching alveolar ridge, voiced
bathe	blaze
clothe	close
rather	razor
leather	laser
smooth	shoes
sooth	use
gather	gazette
rather	rose

Pronunciation of London Underground stations and place names

The most commonly mispronounced stations.
B27

🎧 *Listen and repeat.*

1. Aldgate /ˈɔːlgeɪt/
2. Balham /ˈbæləm/
3. Borough /ˈbʌrə/
4. Clapham /ˈklæpəm/
5. Gloucester Road /ˈglɒstə/
6. Hainault /ˈheɪnɔːt/
7. Holborn /ˈhəʊbən/
8. Leicester Square /ˈlestə/
9. Marylebone /ˈmærələbən/, /ˈmærələbəʊn/, /ˈmɑːlɪbəʊn/
10. Plaistow /ˈplɑːstəʊ/
11. Ruislip /ˈraɪslɪp/
12. Southwark /ˈsʌðək/
13. Theydon Bois /ˈθeɪdən ˈbɔɪz/
14. Tottenham Court Road /ˈtɒtnˌəm/
15. Uxbridge /ˈʌksbrɪdʒ/
16. Vauxhall /ˈvɒksɔːl/

Some of the most commonly mispronounced London place names:
B28

🎧 *Listen and repeat.*

1. Aeolian Hall /iːˈəʊlɪən/
2. Beaucham Place /ˈbiːtʃəm/
3. Cadogan Place /kəˈdʌgən/
4. Chiswick /ˈtʃɪzɪk/
5. Geffrye Museum /ˈdʒefriː/
6. Greenwich /ˈgrenɪdʒ/, /ˈgrenɪtʃ/
7. Isleworth /ˈaɪzəlwəθ/
8. Madame Tussauds /ˈmædəm tʊˈsɔːdz/
9. Woolwich /ˈwʊlɪdʒ/, /ˈwʊlɪtʃ/
10. Conduit Street /ˈkɒndjʊɪt/

Pronunciation of British place names

The following are some of the most commonly mispronounced British place names.

B29

🎧 *Listen and repeat.*

1. Alnwick Castle /ˈænɪk/
2. Beauvoir /ˈbəʊvwɑː/
3. Bicester /ˈbɪstə/
4. Belvoir Castle /ˈbiːvə/
5. Berkshire /ˈbɑːkʃə/
6. Carlisle /kɑːˈlaɪl/
7. Derby /ˈdɑːbiː/
8. Edinburgh /ˈedɪnbrə/, /ˈe dnbrə/
9. Fowey /ˈfɔɪ/
10. Folkestone /ˈfəʊkstən/
11. Leicester /ˈlestə/
12. Leominster /ˈlemstə/
13. Maidstone /ˈmeɪdstən/
14. Market Harborough – /ˈmɑːkɪt ˈhɑːbʌrə/
15. Milton Keynes /mɪltən kiːnz/
16. Newquay /ˈnjuːkiː/
17. Norwich /ˈnɒrɪdʒ/, /ˈnɒrɪtʃ/
18. Salisbury /ˈsɔːlzbriː/
19. Slough /ˈslaʊ/
20. Shrewsbury /ˈʃrəʊzbriː/
21. Warwick /wɒrɪk/
22. Wokingham – /ˈwəʊkɪŋəm/

Strong and weak forms chart

The following chart shows some of the most commonly used words which change when in an unstressed position in a phrase or sentence.

B30

Listen and repeat.

Word	Strong form	Weak form
are	ɑː	ə
am	æm	əm
can	kæn	kən
shall	ʃæl	ʃəl
have	hæv	həv or əv or v
had	hæd	həd
were	wɜː	wə
was	wɒz	wəz
and	ænd	ənd
as	æz	əz
at	æt	ət
but	bʌt	bət
for	fɔː	fə
from	frɒm	frəm
her	hɜː	hə
not	nɒt	nt
of	ɒv	əv
that	ðæt	ðət
them	ðem	ðəm
to	tuː	tʊ or tə

Glossary

Articulation - The exercising and thus strengthening of the speech organs to produce sharp, crisp consonants, leading to good clear diction.

Intonation - The gentle rise and fall of the voice in a phrase or sentence.

Inflection - The rise and fall of the voice in a word or syllable.

International Phonetic Alphabet – An alphabet of symbols representing sounds.

Phonetics - The science concerned with the study of speech processes, including the production, reception and analysis of speech sounds.

Voice modulation - Variation in the strength, tone or pitch of one's voice.

Idioms - A group of words whose meaning is different from the meanings of the individual words.

Glottal stop - A sound made when the vocal chords are closed tightly, not allowing air to flow through (like holding your breath or lifting something heavy).

Parenthesis - A word or phrase added as an explanation or afterthought.

The 4 Ps definitions
Pitch - The variety of levels of the height and depth of the spoken voice.

Pace - The speed or rate of speech, ranging between very fast and very slow delivery.

Power - The variable amount of volume used in speaking, from very loud to very soft.

Pause - A short stop or rest in speech, creating a momentary silence.

Bibliography

Bab Ballads, W.S. Gilbert, MacMillan and Co. Ltd., 1935

A Book of Beauty, compiled by John Hadfield, Edward Hulton, 1958

The Doves Nest and Other Stories, K. Mansfield, 1984.

Emlyn Williams Readings from Dickens, William Heinemann Ltd., 1954

English Pronouncing Dictionary, Daniel Jones, Cambridge University Press, 1977

Old Possum's Book of Practical Cats, T.S. Elliot, Faber and Faber Ltd., 1957

An Outline of English Phonetics, Daniel Jones, W.Heffer and Sons Ltd 1955

The Oxford Book of English Verse, Oxford, Clarendon Press, 1900

The Rattle Bag, edited by Seamus Heaney and Ted Hughes, Faber and Faber, 1982

Sound and Sense, Wilton Cole, George Allen and Unwin Ltd., 1942

Speech in Practice, Christabel Burniston, English Speaking Board, 1955

Tales of the Unexpected, H.G. Wells, Collins, 1954

Acknowledgements

This book would not have been what it is without endless support of Michael Knowles, actor and writer who contributed enormously in recording audio and writing our humorous dialogues.

We are immensely grateful for all the hard work done by our chief editor, Bud Smith.

We conducted a number of interviews with English language teachers and they all wanted to have a new book on connected speech patterns. This was a big encouragement to us!

We would like to thank many foreign students from France, Japan, Spain, Germany and India, who helped during our marketing research. A special thank you to Nandita Kamat, who played an important part in preparation of this book.

Cover design by Ben Strawbridge.

Illustrations from *Big Book of Old-Time Spot Illustrations*, Edited by Hayward Cirker.